Preaching Through the Pain

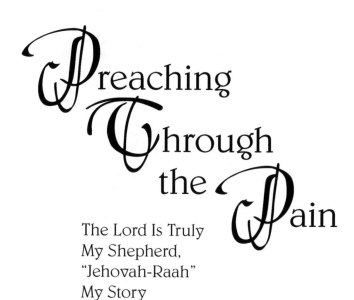

Preaching Through the Pain

The Lord Is Truly
My Shepherd,
"Jehovah-Raah"
My Story

Helen M. Crawford McBynum

WESTBOW
PRESS®
A DIVISION OF THOMAS NELSON
& ZONDERVAN

WestBow Press books may be ordered through booksellers or by contacting:

WestBow Press
A Division of Thomas Nelson & Zondervan
1663 Liberty Drive
Bloomington, IN 47403
www.westbowpress.com
1 (866) 928-1240

Scripture quotes marked (KJV) are taken from the King James Version of the Bible.

ISBN: 978-1-5127-6772-8 (sc)
ISBN: 978-1-5127-7170-1 (e)

Print information available on the last page.

WestBow Press rev. date: 7/21/2017

Contents

DEDICATION

This book is dedicated to my Heavenly Father. I thank
Him for calling, choosing and ordaining me to carry
His Word to the people, I also thank Him for giving
me the Inspiration and strength to write this book.
I could not make this journey without Him but I can
do all things through Christ that strengthen me

A Special thanks to Vidya Ananthanarayanan for assisting with the editing of my manuscript which has resulted in a inspirational book that will encourage others. I appreciate your honesty. You are truly a blessing.

Special thanks to Hervadine Herbin for Author's Photo

Acknowledgments

To my family and friends whom I love dearly, thank you for loving me unconditionally. I know I have made many decisions, done and said things you haven't always understood or agreed with, I want you to know that I understand. I have learned many things on this journey and one of the most important things I've learned is that being obedient to God means that there will be times when others will not understand the instructions He gives to his servants.

My prayer is that you will understand one day. Just remember the One that guides me does not think as we do, and only He knows the plans He has for me. His thoughts and ways are truly not as ours.

"For I know the thoughts that I think towards you,
saith the Lord, thoughts of peace and not of evil,
to give you an expected end" (Jer. 29:11).

A special thanks to Pastor Herbin and First lady (who have become my dearest friends) for accepting me as part of your family. As time passed, we have shared many happy times and each other's pain, but the happy times have out weighted the pain. Both of you have always been by my side because that's what families do.

I know it has not been easy being my Pastor and First Lady and my friend. "Let's just say it's a challenge." You accepted the responsibility of having a woman minister on your staff when most pastors would have refused because you knew before I did that God had called and chosen me. You chose to be obedient to God rather than worry about what others might think.

I will always remember one particular incident, when you introduced me as one of your ministers, and the minister to whom you introduced me to made the statement "that you were one of those pastors". You just ignored the comment and continued to tell him I was an awesome preacher, teacher, I could also pray. I was and I am so proud and happy to be under your leadership.

My sisters and brother thank you both for taking such good care of me, and keeping me focused on what God has called me to do. God has bought us all through a lot of storms.

Thanks for allowing me to be a part of your grandchildren's lives when I needed them the most. You are truly a man and woman of God.

Thank you, Pastor; for taking me under your wing and teaching and training me to be the minister that God would have me to be. You taught me to always preach the uncompromising Word of God; to be obedient to the Holy Spirit. No matter what is said or what man may try to do, I am to stand on the Word of God. I have learned as Paul did, that by myself I can do nothing, but through Christ I really can do all things.

To my oldest godson, who will soon be eighteen years old, thanks for just hanging with me since you were 4 weeks old. Remember to always keep God's Word in your heart and let him be your guide as you get ready to go out into the world. You will find that you will be able to do all things through Christ that gives you strength.

**"I can do all things through Christ which
strengthens me' (Phil. 4:13).**

Preface

Life is a journey, and as we travel on this journey we go through different seasons. One season ends another one begins. Some seasons are easier to go through than others, but there is a set time for each one of us, and there is not a thing man can do to change it. I know that sometimes we think we are changing some things in our lives and we forget that God already know what we are going to do and has already made provisions for us.

This has been a very difficult season of my journey; because for me to write this book has meant that I would have to relive a very painful time of my life. Even though it has been painful, in many ways, it has also been a healing process for me. God let me know that the book wasn't about me, but instead it is about how He worked through me, using me (His vessel) to let His children and the world know that nothing was too hard for Him.

The world need to know that God not only heals a mother's heart that has lost her only child as He has done for me, but that He will heal their broken heart also, replace their pain with the joy of having had their loved one in their lives for a while. He wants the world to realize that everyone that has had a loved one to leave them, He is there to see them through if they allow him to. It doesn't matter what type of heartache or pain, whether it is a husband, wife, child or parent, He is there to get us through.

So, this book is really about God teaching me, using me for his glory and to reach others and draw them to him. I understand now that it was a part of God's plan. When I thought I was healed God let me know that not only was I not healed but the pain I thought I was hiding I wasn't hiding it at all. It was just a form of healing, but now He was going to heal me. I will try to explain it this way.

Have you known someone that had surgery and it seemed to be healing just fine, but they went to the doctor and he examined it he found that it was not healing properly on the inside, therefore he had to open the wound, clean it, so it could heal from the inside out. Whatever was preventing it from healing on the inside had to come out so real healing could take place. Just as the doctor is concerned that surgical wounds heal from the inside out, God want us to be healed from the inside out emotionally and spiritually.

So, it has been with this book, every time I thought I was healed emotionally, God would examine me and find more pain that I had tried to cover up. He would open the wound of my heart where the pain was, and even where my Spirit had been wounded, and show me how to face whatever I needed to accept so that healing for the Spirit and body could take place. I sincerely hope as you read my story you will gather strength from it.

I have learned that whatever God allows us to go through there is a purpose and He will get the glory; He is always right there with us to see us through.

"He healeth the broken in heart, and bindeth up their wounds" (Ps. 147: 3).

I am so grateful to God for allowing my son to be there for my first sermon. You see as I began this part of my journey preaching the gospel, I also soon began a grieving process, I preached my first sermon in January 2005 and God took my son home a couple of months later, in March of 2005, so I was experiencing great joy, and great sorrow simultaneously. At times, I would feel so much joy knowing that God had chosen me as one of his vessels to carry His Word, and then I would feel guilty because I felt so much pain also.

So, with this joy of knowing that God had chosen me, this little quiet person from North Carolina, to stand before the people and deliver His word while experiencing tremendous grief of losing my only child, I didn't know how I would ever get through all of it; but God was and still is leading and guiding me on this journey.

Just as He told Joshua that He would always be with him, He has also let me know that He would always be with me and I didn't have to be afraid, just go forth and do as he had commanded me.

Have not I commanded thee? Be strong and of a good courage; be not afraid, neither be thou dismayed: for the Lord thy God is with thee whithersoever thou goest" (Josh. 1:9)

Introduction

If you are wondering who I am, I am a woman of God with a purpose given to me by God. I know what my purpose is now, and even though there has been, and I am sure there still are many more obstacles before me, mountains to climb and valleys to go through. I now know for sure that:

> *"I can do all things through Christ which strengthens me' (Phil. 4:13).*

You will see that scripture more than once in this book and it is not an error. I hope someone reading this will begin to believe it as I do. I get so much joy and peace just knowing that no matter what He gives me to do, I can accomplish it because I will be led by the Holy Spirit, I will be doing it through Him. When things get too hard I have some place I can also go and that place is in the safety of His arms.

The purpose of this book is to let others know that no matter what our trials are that we may face on this journey that there is nothing that is too hard for our God. He will be with us every step of the way. We just have to put our trust in Him. I hope you will be strengthen as you read the book, He really does give us strength for this journey.

Soon after God called me into the ministry I learned very quickly that there will be those that will put stumbling blocks in your path just because you are being obedient to God. What they didn't know and some still refuse to understand is that when God has chosen you, He has already prepared you and He will make your enemies your footstool, and if you are following Him, he will lead you right over or around those stumbling blocks.

I don't fear man, what they may say or think because I am a minister of the gospel, but I do fear what the consequences would be if I were to disobey God and yield to what man wanted me to do.

"For God hath not given us the Spirit of fear, but of power, and of love and of a sound mind. Be not thou therefore ashamed of the testimony of our Lord, nor of me his prisoner, but be thou partaker of the afflictions of the gospel according to the power of God. Who hath saved us and called us with a holy calling, not according to our works, but according to his own purpose and grace which was given us in Christ Jesus before the world began" (2 Tim. 1:7-9).

I tried to pretend for a little while that I wasn't being called, but after God allowed me to go into the belly of my own fish I gladly accepted my call without fear of what anyone might say or think. My answer to God was a resounding Yes!!!

I have learned that all things work together for our good even though we may not understand it at the time. As God shapes, prunes and mold us for his use, sometimes it may get painful, but He is doing it for our good.

"And we know that all things work together for good to them that love God, to them who are the called according to his purpose" (Rom, 8:28).

CHAPTER 1
A Humble Beginning

I grew up in North Carolina, the third oldest of seven children. My parents were sharecroppers. We lived in the country between two small towns, the larger of the two was Kinston.

We grew up in the church. The country churches held services once a month because in those days usually the Pastors had to drive a long distance to get to their church and they also pastored more than one church, so we attended different denominations.

We went to the Methodist church sometimes on the first Sunday, on the second Sunday we were at my mother's church which was and still is the Disciples Church of Christ, and on the third Sunday we were at the Holiness church.

We loved going there because the people seemed to really have a good time singing and shouting. As children, we didn't understand all that was going on except that they sure were having a good time. They would have something called testimony time.

I asked my mother once if they were so happy about what God was doing for them why were they crying, my mom said because they were happy and they were thanking God for being so good to them. I didn't understand it then but I do now. They were letting their friends and neighbors know that if God had brought them through their storm, He would surely bring them out of theirs.

There were times when we weren't able to go to my mother's church and we would go to the Baptist church that was about a mile from our house. We walked that mile to get to the Church and we were always there in time for Sunday school.

Since we lived in the country, we didn't get out at night very much, so the Baptist church would have prayer meeting on the fourth Sunday instead of during the week, which we attended most of the time.

As I got older most of my friends were attending the Baptist Church so my parents finally allowed my older brother, sister and myself to attend there on the second Sunday, for Sunday school and church.

There was a revival one week and a group of us decide we wanted to join church. The adults were so happy that so many young people were coming into the church. My mother had given her approval but I always felt that she had hoped that we would choose her church.

I remember vividly the Saturday that I was baptized, it seemed as if there were about twenty of us and we were all dressed in white wading out into the murky water for the deacons to baptize us. I remember I wasn't afraid because we had been taught and my mom had told me that Jesus was also baptized.

As the group of us were going into the water which I called a river, to be baptized the mothers and deacons of the church were singing the hymn "Take me to the water to be baptized" I'll never forget it, I felt really good when we came out of the water and I remember thinking to myself that I just wanted whatever my mom and her friends had, and maybe one day I would want to testify and cry because I would be happy too.

After we united with the church I started singing in the choir and ushering with the junior ushers.

One reason my mom allowed us to join another church was she knew if we were disobedient we would be corrected on the spot by an adult, plus they would tell our parents and we wouldn't be able to be with our friends anymore on Sunday. I still try to attend a couple of those churches as often as possible when I go home.

Even though I didn't know it at the time, the young man that would become my husband also attended the same church I united with.

I didn't leave home until I got married. My husband and I attended the same church and same school; he graduated before I did because he was a few years older. We started dating after he went into the military. He was my first love. I had always wanted children, but was having problems carrying a baby full term, but after several miscarriages we finally had our son. We traveled extensively because of the military and finally retired in San Antonio.

I had some wonderful years with my husband and son but nothing could compare to the feeling I had on the day I accepted my calling into the ministry and the day I preached my first sermon. It was and still is a joy and peace that I cannot explain.

So, there we were that Sunday in January of 2005, with family and friends, I had just finished my first sermon, God let me know he was pleased, and I was so happy I cried.

Now I fully understood why the saints were shouting and crying, for it was truly a time for praising and giving thanks to Him.

I have learned we should always praise God and let our loved ones, family and friends know that we care because we never know when it will be the last time we see them or hear their voice. God is the only one that knows our future and the plans He have for us. What we think our future is going to be is usually totally different from the plan He has already put in place. I am so glad He does not think as man thinks.

We know that the Bible tells us that his ways and thoughts are not like ours.

"For my thoughts are not your thoughts, neither are your ways my ways, saith the Lord. For as the heavens are higher than the earth, so are my ways higher than your ways and my thoughts than your thoughts" (Is. 55:8-9).

We don't always understand what God does or how and why He does certain things the way he does but we do know that He's working it for our good.

CHAPTER 2
Beginning of a New Season

Some years ago, and this was in the late 1990's, I was in my wash room putting clothes in the washer. I had just gotten off the phone with the manager of a bank about a job. I had sent out several resumes and she had called me to see if I was interested in a part- time position as a teller, because even though she was impressed with my experience and my resume, all they had to offer was a part time position. At the time I was out of work. I had been employed for many years with a financial institution, but because of the difficulties some of them were having they were being acquired by other banks which resulted in downsizing the staff. As a result I was given early retirement. I informed her that I would give her my answer the next day because I really needed a full time position.

I learned very quickly that when it seems as if you have been handed one of the worst breaks in your life, when a door has been slammed shut in your face, that God has something bigger and better planned for you. As I continued putting the clothes in the washer and talking to God, telling him I didn't know what else to do, I remember saying, God you know I can't make it on a part time job, not realizing he was getting ready to show me how to make it without a job at all until he decided to give me one.

A little later I continued to put more clothes in the dryer and God begin to speak to me, He told me that he had chosen me, He didn't tell me all that he had in store for me to do, just that He had chosen me.

I must admit that I was startled or maybe scared is a better word, to say the least when I heard this voice and I was in my home alone. As he spoke I was afraid to say anything. I quickly turned off the washer, I'm not sure if I turned it off so I could hear clearly or if I wanted to make sure that I was really hearing this voice. I can tell you his voice was clear and soft, a voice I had never heard before and one I will never forget. For a while I didn't even move and when I did I remember I just started crying. I just felt really good, and happy. I remember thinking later how can I feel this good and I don't even have a job.

I can tell you when your only income is your retirement pay and when you had no intention of retiring for a long time it doesn't cover your bills for very long, that's why when God instructed me not to look for a job anymore because he had work for me to do. It took me the rest of the day to accept the fact that I better do as I was told, as a matter of fact I was afraid not to.

You see, I had gone to the store earlier in the week and purchased this fancy resume paper to start typing my resume on, hoping that maybe it would impress people but after the encounter with God I just put it aside in a safe place as a reminder of that day.

Even though I didn't have a job I received some money, God gave me a job so that he would get the glory and I would be blessed beyond measure. He began to teach me to totally trust him, have faith and obey him.

He used me to help others and I learned then what my mom had always told me and that is, that you don't have to have a lot of money to help others. Once my neighbors realized I wasn't working they would share their food with me. God was just blessing me so that I could be a blessing to others.

Since I was not working I now had more time to visit my neighbor more that was ill and take her places, to babysit when needed. I was now available to help others in need.

I must tell you when God opened the door for the job He had for me, it was something I had never dreamed of and it was not a job I had applied for, it was a job that He opened for me through someone He used in the church and if there ever was a perfect job that was it. All at once I had a job I hadn't applied for, I also had an office and had opportunity to hire whomever I thought would be a good assistant. We truly serve an awesome God.

If you don't get anything else out of this book, I want everyone to please remember this, don't ever give up on God, if He said it He will do it. God promised me that he would always be with me and to just trust him that He would work miracles in my life and He has done just that and He is still doing it... If only I had the time to tell you some of the miracles He has performed in my life.

Through all my heartaches and pain, trials and tribulations I have learned to trust and depend on Him and I wouldn't change anything even if I could; because everything that I have been through and everything the enemy has tried to do has made me draw closer to God.

When I lost my son, Satan thought that was a perfect opportunity for him but he was and still is a liar. He would tell me if God loved me He would have healed my son instead of letting him die, and now I had no one, he even used people to tell me that now you don't have anybody. Don't get me wrong, I don't think they meant any harm for they were telling me something I had already told myself, but we were both wrong because God was and still is with me and He will never leave or forsake me.

During the time when I wasn't working there was always food on my table and enough gas in my car to go where He wanted me to go. He is an awesome God. Through it all I learned to trust and lean on Him.

CHAPTER 3
Why the Book? Assurance and Obedience

I f I was to receive the healing I needed, I had to do what God had called me to do and follow his instructions. He instructed me to write this book. I would like to assure and reassure everyone that read this book that our God is an awesome God. He keeps his promises. He is a protector and a keeper. He protects and keeps us even from ourselves when necessary, and when we feel that we don't even want to be kept. What I mean by that is, He will keep us even when we think in our carnal mind that we don't want to be kept, that we can handle things on our own.

There are times in our lives that we are in such a dark place that we don't even want to be kept. When our hearts are breaking and grief, sorrow and all kinds of troubles seen too much to bear and we just want to give up, I'm so glad that God looks at and knows our heart; that even as we are grieving and going through other types of pain He will keep us and let us know that He is there, and that He sees our tears and hears our cries. We have the assurance that in times of our distress if we call on Him he will hear us and come to our rescue.

"In my distress I cried unto the Lord and he heard me" (Ps. 120:1).

To go through any type of pain is a process, but the loss of a child is a special kind of pain and we have to allow God to heal us.

his way, I can assure you that He can and will restore you and give you the strength to go on just as he did David.

> *"He restoreth my soul; He leads me in the path of*
> *righteousness for his Namesake" (Ps. 23:3).*

and He also lets us know that:

> *He healeth the broken in heart and bindeth*
> *up their wounds" (Psa. 147:3).*

We are his children just as David was and if he would restore David's soul he will do the same for us. We have been adopted into his family; so all we have to do is be patient and wait on him. There is nothing too hard for him. We just have to step out of the way and let God direct our path. As he heals us he walks with us and strengthens us as we go through the valley of shadow of death. When we feel we can't make it another day, he will renew our strength.

> *"Has thou not known/ hast thou not heard, that the everlasting*
> *God, the Lord, the Creator of the ends of the earth, fainteth not,*
> *neither is weary? There is no searching of his understanding.*
>
> *He giveth power to the faint, and to them that have no might*
> *he increaseth strength. Even the youths shall faint and be*
> *weary, and the young men shall utterly fall. But they that*
> *wait upon the Lord shall renew their strength, they shall*
> *mount up with wings as eagles: they shall run and not be*
> *weary: and they shall walk and not faint" (Is., 40: 28-31).*

So in obedience to God I sat down and began to write, to go on my journey of healing even though I didn't know where it would take me or the process that God had chosen for me. One thing I did know for sure and that was I did and still do trust Him.

CHAPTER 4
Why this Title for The Book?

To understand this book, I ask you to take "<u>Note</u>" of the title which is "Preaching through the Pain". It doesn't mean that I'm still carrying all the pain and preaching, but that I am going through the pain and it gets less painful as time goes by. It's not just the pain of losing my son but also the pain that goes with being a minister called by God into his ministry in a Baptist church where there is much hostility against women ministers.

I learned very quick that God put us where he wants us to serve, we don't have a choice because it is not about us, no matter what we may be going through in our personal lives he has already made provisions for us.

I am encouraged everyday by the many anointed women of God that have touched my life, and I see them carrying the Word of God to the world as God has instructed them. God has strengthened me for this journey and has dressed me with His whole armor, so no matter what is said or done I will always stand on His Word and be obedient.

You might ask why I say that I'm preaching through the pain; I say that because I found that there are different levels of grief, of pain, and it's different I believe for everyone because of the simple fact that we all handle the stages of our lives differently.

I have learned that people in general do not like to talk about death very much but we know that death touches us all eventually; someone we love departs this world, it's part of "the journey," a part of life.

The Bible tells us in Psalm 23 that there is a valley of the shadow of death, but we can't stay there we have to go through it because if we don't it will consume us even while we are still alive.

Very often when we lose a loved one people say the wrong thing while trying to give comfort because they do not really know what to say. I can tell you that sometimes it is ok not to say anything, just being there for that person means more than words can say.

I have come through the pain and grief by spending time with God, trusting him, by praying and preaching His Word. After the pain and grief, then came " just pain" that is the only way I can describe it. All I can tell you is that through much prayer and fasting, being committed to my God, still praising him, loving him, trusting him and striving to do his will in spite of that pain is what has brought me this far. I had to allow Him to guide me through that valley, trusting that he would surely deliver me out of that pain and believe that everything I was going through was for my good and by His grace and mercy I have come through.

I can tell you that the pain I felt at one time made my heart hurt so, that I thought at times it would burst, but that kind of pain is gone now, and has been replaced with a peace that I cannot explain. There is sort of a dull ache I feel sometime but the peace that God has given me pushes the heartache and sadness away and replaces it with happy memories of my son.

You may ask, do I miss my son? The answer is yes, everyday; and there are times that it seems as if it just happened, but God always quickly replaces it with good memories of my son and remind me of the boys (my godchildren) that he has placed in my life and the reason that I am in theirs.

He reminds me of my purpose as his vessel and what He has called me to do and nothing can hinder that purpose.

"Yea though I walk through the valley of the shadow of death I will fear no evil for thou art with me, thy rod and thy staff, they comfort me" (Ps. 23:4)."

CHAPTER 5

The Mother and the Preacher

When I first started to write this book, I didn't think I would be able to do it; it would be too painful, but God reminded me that this wasn't just a book, it was a true story, a message to mothers all over the world and fathers that has lost a child and especially their only child. I put emphasis on only child because Kenny was my only child. There may not be a difference whether it is the only child or not but I can tell you for sure how it feels to lose your only child.

My prayer is that this book will help others that are grieving or know someone that is grieving over the loss of their child, whether it is their only child or if they have other children. I hope they will learn what I have, and that is, that God will see you through if you just trust Him. I hope that they will realize that as humans we will go through what we think are unbearable situations but God is always with us, and with Him leading the way we will be able to get through it.

As we go through that valley of grief or any type of pain, that dark place where there is so much danger of falling and just staying there, God is there and he will restore us and lead us in the path of righteousness, we are safe with him. Just hold on to God as if your life depends on it, because it really does, He is the only one that can bring you through.

I can honestly tell you that it's just like being a child in your mother's arms being protected until the storm is over. We have a safe place in His arms. We must believe that there is nothing too hard for Him, but you can only do that when you have put your trust in him and realize that we can do nothing without Him.

So, as for me it is imperative that I write this from a personal perspective of a mother that has lost her only child because that has been my experience. I can tell you how God cared for me and is still taking care of me, what He has taught me, how He has wiped my many tears away.

I also write this from the heart of a preacher chosen by God to deliver His Word to the people. He has comforted me and strengthened me and told me to continue to stand before the people and preach, teach and minister to the people.

One thing I can tell you for sure that I learned very quickly, and that is, people expect more from you if you are a minister and lose a child. I can't tell you how many times I heard the words, but you are a minister, you understand that stuff, so you'll be ok." Actually, they were right, I did understand what I did not want to understand, (if that makes any sense). What I mean by that is, I knew deep down in my spirit I was going to be ok because I knew God was going to see me through it, but the mother part of me only knew at the time that my child was gone forever. What I didn't grasp at that time was God also knew that I needed to grieve. It turns out that I was the one that didn't realize I hadn't grieved for my son.

I can tell you what I have gained, what God has taught me, how he told me I would continue to preach His Word, that nothing would hinder me from spreading the gospel to a lost world; that I would minister to the people wherever He sent me. I didn't understand all of what He was telling me then because He had called me into the ministry a couple of years earlier and I had been busy resisting Him instead of listening to Him.

I had received Christ as my Lord and Savior a long time ago but in my wildest dreams did I ever even think of being called to preach the gospel. There was so much and even now so much to learn about our God, so much that He is willing to reveal to us as we grow closer and closer to him.

CHAPTER 6
Doing It God's Way

As I stated in the introduction, when I first started writing this book it was to encourage mothers and fathers that lost (and I don't like the word lost) because we don't really lose them, God just take them back, but when he takes a child home and especially their only child they would need encouragement and strength to continue on.

As time went by and I realized I couldn't finish the book, I began to ask God to please direct me, show me what it was that I was missing that He wanted me to say because he kept telling me the book was not finished yet I could barely write anymore, and finally He just made me stop writing altogether.

You see, I just wanted to get it finished and over with so I wouldn't have to think about losing my son, at least that's what I was telling myself; in fact, when God stopped me and I had to put it away for a while and a while turned into a few years. I couldn't understand why He would not allow me to finish it, but today I understand. It has taken years to get to where I am now, and it has taken years to finish the book.

Then after all the waiting, one-day God told me it was time to finish so here I am in 2014 beginning to complete one of God's projects that he has given me. I don't know how long it will take me but I do know it will be completed when the time is right. I knew God was awesome, however, I can tell you that he is even more awesome than I had ever imagined. As he reveals to us the plans he has for us,it is too wonderful for words. I say that because of what He has done and is doing in my life and how he is using me, words cannot explain. He gives us the revelation as we follow him on this journey trusting in him and his promise. "Only He knows the plans that he has for us."

The word "I" is the key here because I was thinking of myself when I was rushing to finish what God had given me to do. This book is for God to get the glory as it helps others. He has not revealed his entire plan for the book but I do know He will get the glory if it only reaches one person.

I said earlier that I didn't understand why God told me to stop writing the book, Well, he finally gave me the answer. He began to answer questions I had asked, and the ones that were still on my mind. "He really does know what we are thinking.

I had been home to N.C. on vacation and was sitting in the airport waiting for my flight, still not understanding why God had not even allowed me to write anything while I was at home. It seemed to me that I had wasted time because my plan was to do some writing while I was on vacation but didn't accomplish anything. I definitely had writer's block.

Then something happened, and all at once he began to speak to me and answer my questions. He told me the book was not about me; that He had instructed me to write this book so that it would reach the people that He wanted it to touch, that the book was about how he had worked through me and is still working through me and using me (His vessel) to let his children and the world see and know that nothing was too hard for him. The world needed to know that he not only heals a mother 's heart as he had done with me, one whose only son he had taken home, however, that he would heal their broken heart also, replace their pain with the joy of having had that loved one in their life for a period of time.

God wants the world to realize everyone that has had a loved one to leave them He is there to see them through it if they allow him to. It doesn't matter the type of heartache and pain, and if it is a child, husband, wife or parent; he is there to get us through that heartache and pain. He will take you through any type of disappointment, any trials or tribulations that may come your way as long as you trust him.

So, this book is really about God teaching me, using me to reach others, to draw others to Him. I hope those that choose to read this book and are facing the fact or have faced the fact that their love one is not going to walk through the door anymore, that there will be no more phone calls from them, no matter how long they stare at the phone, will do as I have done; keep trusting in God, loving him depending on Him to get you through.

If you have a loved one that is ill or whatever storm you are going through God will see you through, just keep the faith in Him.

I can tell you that once you have accepted the fact that there will be no more cards and gifts on those special days; He will be right there for you, and in the process of time, little by little healing takes place. Whatever your storm or season is that you are going through, put your trust in Him and lean not to your own understanding.

> *"Trust in the Lord with all thine heart, and lean not to thine own understanding. In all thy ways acknowledge him, and he shall direct thy path" (Prov. 3:5-6).*

This book also tells how God has strengthened me for this journey that I am on and how He has taught me that no matter how much my friends and family love me He is the one that I have to totally depend on in the end. Friends and family are only human and sometimes they let you down without meaning to.

He has reminded me that it was Him that got me up in the mornings when I was too sad and lonely to get out of bed because I knew I would not receive my regular phone call or hear the key in my front door again or the voice calling "mom" as he came in.

God gave me His strength to get through those times. Don't get me wrong now, because He used my friends and family to call and make sure I would get up and go to work, but by the time they called he had already reminded me that he was there with me; and in the wee hours of the night when friends and family would be at home with their family, God would make his presence known to me in a such a warm and gentle way.

My relationship with my Father is even closer and stronger than ever. I can now minister to those that have lost a loved one even more effectively, pray for and be with the family as their loved one slowly slip away into that eternal peace. "He is an awesome God."

CHAPTER 7
God Working for my Good

Many times, when God is working things out for our good it doesn't seem like it at the time. Sometimes we encounter some very strong winds and rough waters, but He will calm the waters and wind for us just as he did for his disciples when they were out to sea and the great storm came up, we have to learn to trust him.

> *"And there arose a great storm of wind, and the waves beat into the ship, so that it was now full. And he was in the hinder part of the ship asleep on a pillow: and they awake him, and say unto him, Master, carest not that we perish? And he arose, and rebuked the wind, and said unto the sea "Peace be still". And the wind ceased and there was a great calm" (Mark, 4:37-39).*

This has been a very difficult journey for me, as I knew it would be; you see, I've had to go back to that place and time in my life where there was so much pain, but it has also been a place where I grew stronger and closer to God.

So, going back to that place and time in my life that I didn't want to go, experience a pain that I was trying and still am working my way through was necessary because I knew for healing to really take place it was a journey I had go on and do it God's way.

As I went back and begin to relive the time of my son's death along with other types of pain I had endured, I found that there were issues that I thought I had gotten past but realized that I had just tucked them away in another part of my heart. I realized there was a pain I had pretended wasn't there so I could get through all of this; forgetting for a moment that I wasn't getting me through anything, that it was only by the grace of God and his love for me that was getting me through.

All these things I thought I had conquered I now had to face them again.

This whole experience, the most painful time of my life that I had tried to forget, all of this I would now have to face on this journey, this season of my life. To say that I didn't want to do this would be an understatement, but God had spoken.

"Shall not God search this out? For he knoweth the secrets of the heart"(Ps. 44:21).

Man looks on the outside but God sees what is on the inside of us. We may hide things from ourselves and others when they are too difficult to face but God knows all our secrets, there is nothing we can hide from him and no place we can go that he is not there. David acknowledges this in Psalm 139: 1-10) when he talks about the presence and power of God.

I've had other losses in my family, my father and mother, and a brother has gone home. I even did the eulogy for my brother, but this was another kind of pain, a pain I never experienced before and I can't describe it.

When God took my mother, I thought there can be no greater pain but I was wrong. A mother always feels connected to her child, and when my son passed it felt like something was being torn from the inside of me and there was nothing to stop the pain. This was the baby I carried for nine months. His father and I watched him grow, we nurtured him, taught him right from wrong, to treat others with kindness, taught him who God was and is and now he was gone, yes, this was another type of pain and God had instructed me to write about it, to share the most private and painful moments of my life with the world. But at the time I couldn't understand how this was going to help me, but I kept remembering the scripture in Romans.

> *"and we know that all things work together for*
> *good to them that love God, to them who are the*
> *called according to his purpose" (Rom.8:28).*

All I could say was I don't understand this God but I trust you and as I began to pray and write it began to come clear what his purpose was. One night when I was struggling with some things I didn't want to put in the book God reminded me that it wasn't about me, but what He was doing through me, so I knew I would continue to write until the book was completed.

CHAPTER 8
To be Chosen by God: The Call

"This is my commandment, that ye love one another as I have loved you. Greater love hath no man than this that a man lay down his life for his friends. Ye are my friends, if ye do what so ever I command you. Henceforth I call you not servants; for the servant knoweth not what his lord doeth, but I have called you friends for all things that I have heard of my Father I have made known unto you. You have not chosen me but I have chosen you and ordained you, that ye should go and bring forth fruit and that your fruit should remain: that whatsoever ye shall ask of the Father in my name he may give it to you" (John 15:12-16).

When God called me into the ministry He didn't call me as a Baptist minister, He didn't call me as a woman, but as one of his vessels. He had called and chosen me for his purpose. He called me to preach the gospel, to teach and minister not to only the lost but also to the saved, to the poor in spirit, and to encourage those that need encouragement along the way; to remind everyone who He is, that He is the same God yesterday, today and forever.

I must say that I now understand the saying that I used to hear a lot when I was growing up. I would sometimes sneak and listen to the older folk talking, they would say "people might as well stop running from what God has called them to do" they would be talking about someone they believed had a calling in their life. I guess that is what I was doing, trying to run from God, Well, I can tell you that it didn't work. I should have known better because I know the story of Jonah very well.

The first time God called me to the ministry, I couldn't believe it so I didn't answer. I knew it was his voice because it was the same voice that had talked with me a few years earlier in my wash room. I remember I got up and called one of my sisters in North Carolina and told her and asked her not to repeat it, as if that would erase God's voice from my mind. Two years later He reminded me of my purpose. I became afraid and told my sister *I didn't know* what I was going to do. You see I am a shy person by nature, not one to volunteer to get up in front of an audience, but would willingly work behind the scene. I love the Lord, but I just knew that I would never be able to stand before people and do what He was commanding me to do, especially in a Baptist church. I can now understand somewhat how Moses felt when God gave him the command to go and tell the Israelites that he had been sent by God to bring them out of bondage and tell Pharaoh what God said.

"And Moses said unto God, who am I, that I should go unto Pharaoh, and that I should bring forth the Children of Israel out of Egypt? And God said, certainly I will be with thee; and this shall be a token unto thee, that I have sent thee: When thou hast brought forth the people out of Egypt, ye shall serve God upon this mountain. And Moses said unto God, Behold, when I come unto the children of Israel, and shall say unto them, The God of your fathers hath sent me unto you; and they shall say to me What is his name? what shall I say unto them? And God said unto Moses, I AM THAT I AM: and he said Thus shalt thou say unto the children of Israel, I AM hath sent me unto you." (Exod. 3:11-14).

I had acknowledged and accepted the gifts God had given me, little did I know that he was preparing me for something even greater, and was giving me everything I would need *for* this journey. He had even placed me in the lives of my pastor and first lady, so I could see some of what the life of a minister was like. I even had the opportunity to work in the same office with the first lady for six years.

I encourage everyone to not be afraid when God reveals your purpose to you, just trust Him, He will lead you in the direction that you need to go, just give Him the glory as He uses you to accomplish His will through you. To be called, chosen and ordained by God is the most humbling and highest honor there is.

CHAPTER 9
Accepting the Call

To be called by God is one of the best things that can happen to us. I say one of the best things because the best thing is when he saves us, when we come before him and repent and accept him as our personal savior. Once we do this we are now his vessel, not just a man or woman, we are his vessel that he will use to draw the lost to Him.

Because I had not been obedient to the voice of God he began to allow some things to happen in my life. I felt as if I was in a big whirlwind and couldn't get out of it. I call it being in the belly of my fish. I kept praying and asking God for help, to show me what he wanted me to do other than preach. I knew deep within that I would surrender to him but I kept telling myself I needed more time. He would not answer me until the morning in my prayer room as I lay in the floor crying and praying and when I told him that I was tired of crying tired of praying and not getting an answer, I told him I surrender totally and completely to him and whatever he wanted me to do I would do it, I would preach, teach, minister to the people wherever he sent me, whether it was a few people or a large group. Then He began to speak to me, (I was one happy child of God) telling me not to be afraid, His Spirit would tell me what to say, that he would always be with me. (and yes, I called my sister again and told her the news).

God took me to the book of Joshua and reminded me that just

as he was with Joshua he would always be with me and would tell me what to say and how to say it. He reminded me because of where he was placing me, (in the Baptist church) and to go into the world, that there would be those that did not believe and would not receive me, that I would feel alone many times but I would never be alone, and I was to continue to stand boldly for his namesake and he would always be with me to strengthen, guide and protect me. I soon learned that even though he was protecting me, that did not mean that I would not have storms to go through and be persecuted for his namesake, and feeling alone was an understatement.

The day that I stood behind the pulpit protected by the Holy Spirit and the anointing, for the first time in my life I felt complete and at peace. I was finally where I belonged. Even though I felt nervous and scared there was a calmness I could not explain.

Have I not commanded thee? Be strong and of good courage,
be not afraid neither be thou dismayed: for the Lord thy
God is with thee whither so ever thou goest"(Josh 1:9).

He tells us in his Word that He will supply all our needs.) Matt.6.

I encourage each of you to accept the Purpose God has for you. He is the only one that knows the plans that He has for us. Accept your call.

Now I understood my purpose. There is truly a peace that surpasses all understanding. That is what I felt when I totally submitted to God and accepted my calling that morning in my prayer room. He told me my purpose, it wasn't what I wanted to hear, but I knew I would now be doing what he had prepared me for, plus I never wanted to lose the peace I felt at that moment. He had now called me twice. I didn't want to answer because I knew I would never be able to do what he had called me to do. This time I had no choice but to listen and accept his plan for my life.

That morning on my knees in tears I listened as God told me

I was right, I couldn't do what He had called me to do on my own but it was He that would enable me to do things through Him. I quietly listened as He revealed some of the plans he had for my life. I say some, because I had already learned that God reveals to us that which he wants us to know when he chooses to.

He did tell me that he would always be with me, and when things got difficult I was to just trust Him and the Holy Spirit would always teach and guide me in the way He would have me to go.

CHAPTER 10
The Preparation for the Next Level

As I started to prepare for my first sermon the Lord began to remind me of some things he had told me. One of the things he reminded me of was that He had called and chosen me to preach His Word, and that there would be times I would feel alone. There would be ridicule, *pain and* disappointment just because of who I was, (his vessel called by him,) but certain people would only see the natural person, a woman; but He had chosen me and He was sending me out into the world as His vessel. It was not about me but what He was going to do through me, that it was not me they hated but the Christ they saw in me. God also reminded me that even he was without honor in his own country, then he told me that he had set my path already, just be obedient to him. After listening to God, I just sat there too afraid to move, thinking "I am going to mess this up".

You know, it's funny but I think sometimes we forget that God is an all- knowing God. He knows what we are thinking whether we say it out loud or not.

It was late that Saturday night before I was to preach my first sermon, I had been in my prayer room, prayed, laid the sermon out before God and gone to sleep, God woke me up about 3: 00 am and talked with me. "Have you ever talked with God in the wee hours of the morning when it's completely quiet" I sat on my couch and God said in his soft but firm voice, remember this, where I have put you, "man can never remove you". I had to and still have to always remember it is not about me but it's all about Him and He has to get the glory, for He is a jealous God. I kept waiting for him to say something else but that was it. As I look back I don't know why I was waiting for God to give me a long speech when I already knew from experience that with me he always speaks soft and quick. I went back to my room and got back into bed and went to sleep, knowing that tomorrow I was beginning the next level that God was taking me to.

CHAPTER 11

Sunday Morning: First Sermon

I t was now the Sunday morning I was to preach my first sermon and as I looked out over the congregation and watched as the people continued to come into the sanctuary I tried not to wonder what they might be thinking. Instead of concentrating on the congregation I started thinking of the scripture in Joshua where God tells Joshua to not be afraid because he would be with him. I knew that God was right there with me. I knew I was as ready as I would ever be, I had accepted what God had called me to do and I would never turn back, I couldn't. We had prayer in my pastor's office and then he left me to be alone with God. My sister joined me shortly after he left out, she asked me if I was ready and I told her yes. We had prayer and then it was time to enter the sanctuary. As I entered, I thought to myself, Wow, there are a lot of people here. I think that was the first time I said the phrase (ok God it's just you and me and you're leading) I say it all the time now.

I was excited as I looked out into the sanctuary and especially happy as I looked at the front row because sitting on those pews were some of my family from North Carolina. My sister and her husband had driven all the way here to be with me at this time. Little did we know that they would soon be back for a not so happy occasion.

Also sitting next to them was my son, my baby, even though he was a grown man he was still my baby. It had been a long time since he had been to church with me but that was ok, because he is here to support me today.

Also sitting in the back of the church were my former-husband and his wife, I wasn't sure if they would be here, but I had invited them because I knew it was important to our son. I was glad they decided to come.

My ex-husband and I had grown up together in North Carolina, attended the same church and knew the same people back home. Even though we were married about twenty-six years, and now divorced we were on good terms. We had known each other most of our lives and we also had a son together. He probably knew me better than anyone else in the building except for our son. No one could have told me that this would be the only time that my son would ever hear me preach, the last time he would ever be together with all the family, that God would soon be taking him home, or that my family would soon return to this same church sit in almost the same spot for a separate occasion.

You see, today I would preach my first sermon at my home church here in San Antonio. I couldn't understand why God would call me at all, why He would choose me of all people and why would He call me into the ministry in a Baptist church when it was very rare that Baptist pastors would even let women participate in devotion and surely they wouldn't allow them to preach in their church; but I had already learned to just trust Him, and he had put me in the care of a wonderful Pastor and First lady.

There were friends from a community organization that I was a part of and they had come to give me support. I had been with this group for many years; we had traveled in and out of the state spreading God's word.

It warmed my heart to see so many familiar faces as I looked around the sanctuary. It was nice to see the people that had come to support me on this, one of the most important days of my life.

Even though I was happy to see everyone that came, the most important person to me that day was my son. He has been through a lot and I'm so proud of him. Most people didn't know that he had been ill for years but still went to college after the military and had a very good job. I just thank God for him.

I remember one day when he was over visiting me (I had cooked of course, always did if I knew he was coming over) and we were talking, and he told me that no matter what he did with his life, his dad and I had raised him to know right from wrong, that sometime people just do things because they feel like it. That made me feel good just knowing that he knew we had raised him right.

The text for my first Sermon was "The Lord is My Shepherd, who is your Shepherd?" I would come to understand later why God had given me that text. I have learned that He truly is my Shepherd; my protector, my provider.

I have totally surrendered my life to God. I am very excited, scared and nervous as I begin this part of my journey with the Lord. I am praying that I don't fail God and just be obedient to the Holy Spirit. Moving to another level in God makes me feel such peace, a type of peace I can't explain.

I knew there were many here today that did not approve of women ministers and had come merely out of curiosity; but there were those that had come to support me and hear the Word preached. I also remember what God had spoken to me the night before, "that where He has put me, man could never remove me.

I had been called by God and after two years of "running" I had finally responded with a loud 'yes Lord" I was tired of trying to not do what I was afraid of and didn't have any idea of how to do it. I wasn't trying to be disobedient to God I just couldn't believe he would choose me when he knew I didn't like to stand before people and talk.

As I said, I was tired. I realized that there was no place I could go that God couldn't see me because he is an all knowing, all seeing God, he is forever present. I was just happy had I finally became obedient. I have learned that God chooses the most unlikely people to go forth in his name.

"O Lord, thou hast searched me, and known me. Thou knowest
my down sitting and my uprising, thou understandest my thought
a far off. Thou compassed my path and my lying down, and art
acquainted with all my ways. For there is not a word in my tongue,
but, lo O Lord, thou knowest it altogether. Thou hast beset me
behind and before, and laid thine hand upon me. Such knowledge
is too wonderful for me; it is high; I cannot attain unto it. Whither
shall I go from thy spirit? Or whether shall I flee from thy presence?
If I ascend up into heaven, thou art there: if I make my bed in hell,
behold, thou art there, if I take the wings of the morning, and
dwell in the uttermost part of the sea; Even there shall thy hand
lead me, and thy right hand shall hold me" (Ps.139, 1:1-10).

I was so happy and thankful that God still wanted to use me. I was still afraid but I had repented for not obeying him the first time he called me. He forgave and reassured me that He would give me the words that he wanted to say to the people and he would always be with me.

I had been preparing for my sermon all week, praying, and seeking God's guidance. He led me to the 23rd Psalm, and gave me my text from the very first verse. (The Lord is My Shepherd I shall not want.) I had no idea that God had given me that sermon to preach because I would need it soon to comfort me as I went through my own valley.

I remember so clearly God coming to me one night in my prayer room and he spoke ever so softly and told me that he had called me, chosen me and already Ordained me before I even knew who I was. He told me how difficult it was going to be at times, but that he would always be with me. He directed me to Deut.: 31 where Moses was giving Joshua instructions; and I knew that if he protected Moses and Joshua he would always be with me to protect me because I belonged to him also. I had been adopted into the family and sealed by the Holy Spirit.

*"And Moses called unto Joshua, and said unto him in the sight
of all Israel, Be strong and of a good courage: for thou must
go with this people unto the land which the Lord hath sworn
unto their fathers to give them; and thou shalt cause them
to inherit it. And the Lord, he it is that doth go before thee,
he will be with thee, he will never fail thee, neither forsake
thee: fear not, neither be dismayed: (Deut. 31:7-8)."*

I realized God had called me not just to stand behind a pulpit
and preach the gospel, that just as He had called Joshua to lead the
Israelites into the promised land He had called me to help lead the
world back to Him. What I mean by that is, that He had chosen me
as He had many others to be a vessel that He would use to bring the
lost world back to Him so they could be reconciled back to Him. I
didn't know it then but no matter what happened in my life I would
always stand and preach, teach, and minister to the lost, wounded,
weary, discouraged Christians, non- Christians and all that would
hear; that no matter what trials and tribulations I might encounter
I would always stand and preach God's Word even though I might
be going through a painful Situation.

Jesus reminded the disciples that He chose them not the
other way around, and He reminds us that he has chosen us, yet
in choosing us He has also given us the freedom to choose or
reject Him.

When choosing to say yes to God we have to make sure we
are willing to go all the way. He tells us if the world hates us just
remember it hated him first. Christ is letting us know in "verse 18"
that we would have to stand and proclaim his Word even among
the enemies and sometime in painful situations as well as when we
are going through our personal storms.

*If the world hate you, ye know that it hated me before it hated
you. If ye were of the world the world would love his own. But*

> **because you are not of the world, but I have chosen you out of the world, therefore, the world hateth you. (John 15: 18-19). KJV.**

All these thoughts were going through my mind as I sat in the pulpit that Sunday morning.

The Holy Spirit was in this place today; the choir sang to the glory of God. Pastor was up to introduce me for the first time, and I had a feeling I had never experienced before.

The Holy Spirit took control and used me today. Even though it was my first sermon I knew I was finally where I belonged. I had been searching for something a long time and didn't know what it was, but now I knew. I had been searching for my purpose in God. Even though I didn't want to accept it when He first called me I now knew I was on my way home.

When the services were over so many people came to me to tell me they were praying for me and the sermon was good. I asked my son what he thought of the sermon and he said" mom you have been preaching a long time you just didn't know it. I just hugged him and smiled. It had truly been a beautiful day. I will always hold close to my heart the words my son spoke to me because he had no idea that what he said was true, that God had called me two years earlier.

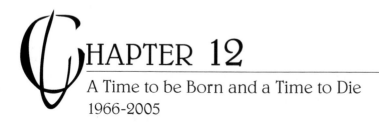

CHAPTER 12
A Time to be Born and a Time to Die
1966-2005

"To everything there is a season and a time to every purpose under the heaven. A time to be born and a time to die; A time to plant and a time to pluck up that which is planted. A time to weep and a time to laugh, a time to mourn and a time to dance" (Eccl., 3:1-2,4).

The Bible tells us that there is a time for everything under the heaven, even a time to die. We all know that we can't live forever, and we have been taught as a child that God never makes a mistake and we know that it's true. But, oh when that death angel comes and take one of our own, for a little while we forget some things that we know are true. For a little while we don't want to think of what we have been taught, we just want to not have that pain. We say to ourselves, I just can't do this and we are right, we can't get through it on our own, but God can get us through it. We have to allow him to lead us. I can tell you by following him you will come through every storm that he allows to come in your life. I have learned that even though it might be the right time for God's will, it doesn't mean that we think in our heart that it's the right time when it happens to one whom we love so dearly.

Sometimes God will reveal some things to us and we might not want to accept them at the time but it doesn't mean that we don't understand. It's one of those times when we say to ourselves I understand but I don't want to understand. And later as we come out of the storm God will reveal even more to us.

I've had other loses in my family, both my mother and father and a brother. I even did the eulogy for my brother.

I remember when God took my mom home I thought there was no greater pain because Your mother was supposed to always be there for her children, and I felt lost without her.

I was wrong about the pain. The greatest pain for me was when God took my son home and I had no say in the matter. We are talking about my baby, the one I carried for nine months inside my body, that I had nurtured, loved, trained, and watched grow into a young man. I had kissed his little wounds and made it better, corrected him when he was wrong.

Yes, this was a different type of pain.

No matter what anyone said or did he was gone from this world. He was really dead and that was a fact and there was nothing I could do to change that.

I knew, and had read in the Bible that there is a time to live and a time to die, but I can tell you it is altogether another story when one has to accept it.

CHAPTER 13
The Phone Call No One Wants to Receive

The telephone rings and we answer without a second thought, not realizing that it could change our lives forever.

That Monday started out just like any other Monday and it ended as the way another day will never end. I went to work as usual, I was only working part time now; because of the war my job on base was slowly being phased out, I had gone from having an office with a full time office employee to a part time technician; now I was the only one in the office and my hours were now 20 hours a week instead of 40 and I had a part time technician. I will always believe the recession had started long before it was officially declared a recession.

Kenny, his real name was Kenneth, " but I only called him that when I was really upset with him" Kenny had spent most of the weekend at my house, which he usually did unless he had plans. He had this idea that he was supposed to make sure I was ok, plus I always cooked.

It's funny, but to him I was **never** supposed to get mad or upset "unless it was him making me upset then that was ok, I think it is a mom –son thing. It's funny, how kids whether adult or still a child, they *always want to know where their parents are, what's going* on with them but don't think we should know where they are or what they are doing, especially the adult children.

Kenney left my home and went to work that Sunday evening as

usual. He always went to work even if he wasn't feeling well and he was very seldom late. He worked nights so it wasn't unusual that I didn't hear from him on Monday because he usually called about the middle of the week.

Most people will tell you that they do not like to get late night or early morning phone calls because it usually means bad news. But I am here to tell you bad news can come any time of the day or night and my call came late in the afternoon. It's funny how one phone call can change one's life so drastically.

It was around six o-clock on a cool evening in March when I received a call from my former husband asking if I had talked to Kenny during the day, I just said no but he should be at work. When he told me that Kenny's boss had called him because Kenny had not shown up at work and he wanted to know if he was ill, because he had not called which was unlike Ken, plus he rarely missed work. That's when my life was changed forever. I knew in my heart that something was very wrong. When his dad said he was on his way to his apartment I told him I would meet him there. As I got dressed I had this strange feeling inside me and it scared me. I can't explain to you my readers, but I knew my world as I had known it was over; that something was happening and I had no control over it.

Kenny had been ill for years. Before he got out of the military he started having seizures and was later diagnosed with epilepsy. The doctors weren't sure why, but today as I listen to the news I wonder if it came from the concussions he got while playing football in high school. He still went to college and had a good job.

When I look back I didn't think to get the key to his apartment because I just assumed he was at home not feeling well, as a result neither one of us had the key to his door and had to get the apartment manager to open the door.

I won't even try to tell you what happened when we got to his apartment, it is still too painful, but I can tell you about a star, Pete called my attention to it, there was the brightest and biggest star that I have seen and it seem to just hover over his apartment complex and both his dad and myself somehow knew at that moment he was gone. His dad told me to go home so I left, knowing in my heart that I would soon receive another phone call. I don't remember driving home I only remember Pete calling to tell me our baby was gone; I remember calling my pastor's home and one of my sisters and she called the rest of my family. I don't remember when I slept but I remember just repeating God help me.

I don't know if anyone will believe this but it's true, every night for about a year I would go outside and that star that we saw at my son's apartment would be there separated from the other stars and shining so bright. Then one night I was on my way home and I looked up couldn't see the star anymore. I don't know why but I was so upset it seemed as if my heart was breaking all over again. I understand now that I had made myself think that as long as I could see the star that looked like the one we saw the night Kenny died it was as if he had not completely gone. Knowing he was gone and accepting it was two different things.

CHAPTER 14
When Everyone Goes Home

Time waits for no man. Life goes on no matter what happens in our lives and that includes when God takes a loved one home. The sun still rises every morning and goes down every evening, the hours, minutes and seconds still go by without stopping.

After the services for my son I knew my family and friends had to go home so I encouraged them to go plus I knew I needed to be alone. Now I didn't say I wanted to be alone, I said I needed to be alone and I knew no one could protect me from what was to come. When my friends began to leave, it hurt so much to see the pain in their eyes, and I tried to reassure them I would be ok.

I thank God for my friends that God had already placed in my life here in San Antonio. Through them and the constant calls from my family I was reminded that I needed to sleep and eat, they watched over me. Sometime God will send angels to watch over you.

I knew going back to work was the best thing for me. My office was located in a area on the military base that I could have my privacy yet I was not totally alone. What I didn't realize was that God was revealing to my pastor that I could not be allowed to become idle at this trying time in my life. The first Sunday I was back at church my pastor asked me to sing a solo, I can't sing that well but it was a song God gave a long time ago to see if I would be obedient. (Something is bound to happen when you pray). Two Sundays later he told me it was my turn to preach at the eleven o'clock service. (Oh, yes, my pastor was and is obedient and bold enough in the Lord to put a woman minister up to preach at the 11:00 o'clock hour. I understand now that if I had taken time off (which is what I wanted to do I would have been overcome with grief).

God always know what is best for us. Everything that he allows in our lives, all our trials and tribulations, our heartaches and pain make us stronger in him. It teaches us how to completely put all our trust in him. He already knows how strong we are and when we are at our weakest point, so he gives us strength when we are weak; and with his strength there is nothing we can't overcome.

The scripture tells me that:
"I can do all thing through Christ which strengthen me. (Phil. 4:13).

There were times when I didn't feel like going to work but didn't dare stay home. I soon learned to take it one hour at a time, and as time went by I learned to go from taking it one hour at a time to a day and then a week and a month. No it wasn't easy but every morning in my prayer to God I would ask for strength for the day, and he always heard me. I learned to take it one day at a time and not worry about tomorrow. I was reminded of the scripture in the gospel of Matthew, Christ teaches us not only about fasting and praying but also he tells us not to worry about what tomorrow may bring.

"Therefore I say unto you, take no thought for your life, what ye shall eat, or what ye shall drink; nor yet for your body, what ye shall put on. Is not the life more than meat, and the body than raiment? Wherefore, if God so clothes the grass of the field which today is, and tomorrow is cast into the oven, shall he not much more clothe you, O ye of little faith? Therefore, take no thought, saying, What

shall we eat? Or What shall we drink? or where withal shall we be
clothed. (for after all these things do the Gentiles seek:) for your
heavenly Father knoweth that ye have need of all these things.
Take therefore, no thought for the morrow, for the morrow shall
take thought for the things of itself.... " (Matt. 6:25,30-31,32,34).

CHAPTER 15
Convinced Myself

I thought I was doing fine, at least that's what I had been telling myself. One day God reminded me that I wasn't fine. I was too concerned about what people would say and think, that I had not grieved for my son and I had to do that before I could go forward. He let me know I was trying to heal myself which was impossible to do.

It was then that I realized that I had been going through the motions of allowing him to heal my broken heart, to move the pain I was feeling. I had been holding on to my grief. I also realized that I had been doing what I would tell the congregation not to do when they came to the altar for prayer. I would tell them not to hold on to their burdens, give them to the Lord; leave them at the altar and yet that was what I had been doing with my grief. I had handed over a lot of things to God but I hadn't given him my grief. I had tucked it away and hadn't given it to Him yet, but that night when I asked Him to move the pain and heal my heart, I gave it to Him for real and the healing process began.

He then told me to complete the book. So I am now writing as he guides me. He told me I was trying to be strong, even at this season of my life because that is what I thought was expected of me because I was a minister. I had been told on several occasions by people that I would be ok because I was a minister and I believe the people believed it. (It was I that was having the problem), and deep in my spirit I knew it, it was the carnal man that had the problem.

God told me that there could be nothing that would hinder me from committing myself totally to the purpose in which he had called me. He told me he would, and only He could heal, move the pain and that I had a right to mourn my son, but I didn't have the right to think I could do it on my own.

It was and is not easy being a minister under any circumstances; but those of us that labor in this calling would not change it for anything. God did not say it would be, but he did say he would always be with us.

So being a minister in a Baptist church, a woman and I was new in the ministry, I didn't want to do anything to make the members think that I wasn't qualified to be where God had placed me. I was forgetting for a moment that I had already been qualified by God; and forgetting for a little while because of so much pain and grief that I was experiencing at the time, what God had told me the night before my first sermon; that I had been called, chosen and ordained by him and where He had put me no man could remove me. I forgot for a moment the scripture where he tells us to come unto him, all that are burden and heaven laden and he will give us rest. I forgot for a moment that nothing was too hard for him, that he was and is the "Great I Am".

It was only a few weeks after the funeral when God had reminded me of who I was, and to whom I belonged. I was his vessel that had been called and chosen by him. Every time I felt myself slipping to a sad place God would be right there, and when I would cry out for him, He would pull me out of that horrible pit.

Through much fasting and praying, and just being in the presence of the Lord, he revealed so many things to me. He showed me that it was I that was expecting more of myself because I had allowed a few people to dictate to me how they thought I should act and feel, and along the way I had forgot what He had told me. He reminded me once again who I was and to whom I belonged and why I had been called.

My brothers and sisters, we make life so hard for ourselves

sometimes because we forget what God has promised us as his children and as his vessels. We think we should do some things ourselves instead of just giving it to the Master. We get caught up in what people think of us instead of striving to please God by being obedient to Him.

I know sometimes we think God is not moving fast enough for us and we want to take matters into our hands, but I can tell you it will not work. We have to realize that God is never late and he already knows our struggle, He just wants us to trust Him.

He has a purpose for each of us. He didn't promise it would be easy but He tells us that He would never leave or forsake us. Sometimes our burdens, storms, or whatever type of heartache and pain we are going through, we have a tendency to forget what God has said in his Word.

I have learned so much about myself. I have learned that when much is given much is required. When we get weary along this journey we have a place to rest and gain more strength through him. The gifts that he gives us are not for ourselves, but are to be used when instructed by Him and for him to get the glory.

God knows what each of his children can endure. He has carried me, taught me and revealed so many things to me about me and about who He is and his plans for me, I know my purpose now.

I sincerely hope that as you have been reading my story, you have gathered strength from it. Through all of this, I have also learned that whatever God allows us to go through on this journey, there is a purpose for it and he will never leave us alone to bear it by ourselves. He is always there to guide us through every storm, every heartache, pain and trial that we go through. Only God can take away the pain, but we have to allow him to do so. It's ok to cry, to mourn a loved one, to ask questions when we don't understand, don't know what to do. He will give us an answer. Moses asked God a question when he told him to go to the Israelites and tell them he had been sent to bring them out of Egypt, and to tell Pharaoh to let his people go. Moses wanted to know who shall I say sent me and God answered him.

> *"And God said unto Moses, I AM THAT I AM: and he said, Thus shalt thou say unto the children of Israel. I AM hath sent me unto you. And God said moreover unto Moses, Thus shalt thou say unto the children of Israel, The Lord God of your fathers, the God of Abraham, the God of Isaac and the God of Jacob, hath sent me unto you:...."(Exod. 3:14-15).*

After all, we are human and he already knows our heart and what we are thinking.

> *"I cried unto the Lord with my voice, and he heard me out of his holy hill. I laid me down and slept, I awakened, for the Lord sustained me" (Ps. 3:4-5).*

CHAPTER 16
Grieving on the Inside

No one can tell another how to grieve for a loved one that God has taken back. For each person it is probably different. One thing I have learned and that is, no matter who you are, or what your relationship is with God you still have to take time to grieve, and you need all the love and support you can get. As ministers, we also need the same love and support that we give to others.

The Bible tells us that there is a time to die. As I read that scripture one day I became painfully aware of what I already knew, and that was, that our lives are full of seasons; and God has a plan for each of us as we go through those seasons.

The funeral was beautiful. I was really touched by all of his co-workers that came. Many times young people do not like to attend funerals, not to mention the fact that they offered and wanted to be pallbearers. I did not view his body; God had already showed me how I was to remember him. Some of my family didn't understand it but I knew that God knew what was best for *me*.

I didn't realize until much later that I was holding my grief inside; But because I couldn't bear to see the look on the church family's face and others I told myself I had to be strong, at least while in the public eye.

I felt even worse when I saw the pain and sadness in my family and friend's eyes. I knew they were concerned about leaving me by myself and I didn't want them to think I couldn't handle the death of my son; so I tried to put on a brave face for them. When I look back I don't think I was very successful.

I asked myself how could I carry out my responsibilities as a minister if I couldn't handle my own grief, so without realizing it I suffered for over a year and a half. But even in my suffering God still used me.

I can tell you no matter what storms we have in our lives; God will still use you as you go through. He strengthened me to preach, pray for and, minister to others. I would often find myself praying asking God for guidance and strength, and the Holy Spirit would put others on my heart and I would find myself praying for them instead. Then one day as I was seeking God for answers He reminded me that I was His and He had called me for His purpose, and it was good to let the people know that it was ok to grieve for a loved one that you have lost, and as we grieve he is with us. He will give us strength for the journey, and remember His strength is made perfect in our weakness. I have had to and still do ask for strength every day.

He does not mind if we ask him to strengthen us as we go through our storms, no matter what they are.

The Bible tells us that there is a time to live and a time to die. As His children we will continue to live with him even though this fleshy body will go back to the dust from which it was formed. He reminded me that there is a time for everything under the sun, even a time for the mortal body to go back to the dust of the earth. He reassured me that he would always be with me.

To everything there is a season, and a time to every purpose under the heaven. A time to be born and a time to die, a time to plant and a time to pluck up that which is planted" (Eccl. 3: 1-2).

Sometime I think we read and study God's Word, but don't really believe it. The above scripture above tells us that there is a time to live and a time to die but sometimes it seems as if we don't grasp it until God take a loved one home.

As time began to pass, I began to seek answers from God through prayer and fasting. I began to understand what I didn't want to understand, "now that may not make much sense to some, but if someone reading this book has ever not wanted to understand something that was happening to them because it would hurt too much and chose to convince themselves that they didn't understand when they did, then you understand my previous statement." As God gave me more wisdom and understanding of his Word, I had to accept what I already knew and that was, it is a simple truth that there is" a time to be born and a to die." I don't want to sound redundant, but we have to realize that we do not control that time, God does.

No matter who we are, saved or unsaved, that time exist for all of us. We only have our love ones for a season, for some that season is longer than others. When I see and hear of other parents that will never see their child grow up into adulthood, I am so thankful to God that he allowed me to have my son for almost forty years. It does not make the heart ache any less but it does give me a joy that I can't explain.

I read many books on grief and grieving but it didn't really help because I couldn't concentrate on what I was reading., don't misunderstand me, the books were great, I read them later, but the answers I needed at that time had to come from God.

It wasn't until I stood before the congregation one Sunday morning and gave a testimony on how God was giving me the strength to get through every day; that God knows we are going to grieve for our loved ones and he don't mind. But we can't let it consume us and we have to trust him because He always knows what is best for us. I had to let the people know that its ok to ask God to help you to understand; he will give you an answer. After that I knew I was on my way and God was healing me from the inside out.

As I have grown closer and closer to God and he has taken me deeper and deeper into his word I realized that I had not read anywhere in the Bible where God said we could not grieve or that the pain would ever go away completely while we are here in this life, but he does tell us that His grace is sufficient for us and that the time will come when there will be no more pain or sorrow or tears. I came to realize that he will wipe away some tears for us now if we ask Him.

"And God shall wipe away all tears, from their eyes, and there shall be no more death, neither sorrow, nor crying, neither shall there be any more pain; the former things have passed away" (Rev. 21:4).

CHAPTER 17
Surviving the Walk through the Valley

I won't pretend to you that it has been easy going through that valley. I will tell you that even though it was difficult and at times the way was dark, but I had the best guide there is to lead me and I am still led by him, My God knows every turn in that valley, He has the master plan and He was and is the light that I was and always will follow.

So how does one survive the pain of losing their child, and at the same time being attacked on every side all because God has done something that some people don't approve of, and that is "He has chosen a woman" one of his vessel to preach his Word? There were some that I had hoped would support and pray for me but they decided not to. I was disappointed but I didn't have the energy or time to concentrate on it. Some have forgotten that God does not need man's approval for anything. He is God, "The Great I Am."

The only way it has been and still is possible for me to do what he called me to do is by the grace of God and my total dependence on him.

I was a Novice in the ministry when my son died. I had just peached my first sermon and even though my son was gone I still had that yearning to know more and get closer to God. I was so excited because of what God was doing with me and the things He had told me He would do through me. I just couldn't believe the people couldn't see it also.

My Father has taught me so much since those early days. As I said, I was just entering into the ministry but I soon learned that all I had to do was make sure to whatever I was doing that I was in His will and He got the glory.

I know that He has allowed me to go through some things, even the death of my son so I would be able to help others; to testify of his never failing faithfulness, of His grace and mercy and how He really does work things for our good. He really does give strength to the weary, he gives you strength to preach through the pain or whatever you may be going through at the time. He shows us that when we are weak, then He is made strong. When He chose me He already knew what lay ahead for me and that I would learn to totally lean on and trust in Him. He reminded me just as he did Paul when I kept asking him to make the pain and hurt go away, He directed me to these verses:

And he said unto me, My grace is sufficient for thee: for my strength is made perfect in weakness. Most gladly therefore will I rather glory in my infirmities, that the power of Christ may rest upon me. Therefore, I take pleasure in infirmities, in reproaches, in necessities in persecutions, in distress for Christ sake, for when I am weak then I am strong" (2 Cor..12:9-10).

CHAPTER 18
I Wasn't Angry but I Did Ask God Why

I have heard some people say they were angry with God. I urge them to please don't be angry with God and just try to remember that He really does know what is best for all of us. We may not understand the way He does what He does but later on we wil understand it better.

I wasn't angry with God, but as the days passed I did have some questions to ask Him but was afraid of the answer so I didn't ask the questions for a long time; then one morning I woke up crying, and I fell to my knees asking God why and to help me understand. I had also heard that you are not supposed to question God, but I had questions that only He had the answer to.

I have learned that by asking God why, does not mean you don't trust God, it means just the opposite, it means that you trust Him and Him only because He is the only one that has the answers your questions.

Then I remembered reading in Matthew 17 chapter, that the disciples asked Christ questions concerning the man with the child that was a lunatic, and he brought him to Christ because the disciples couldn't cure him and he answered them.

"And then came the disciples to Jesus apart and said, why could not we cast him out? Then Jesus said unto them, Because of your unbelief; for verily I say unto you, if you have

> *the faith as a grain of mustard seed, ye shall say unto this
> mountain, remove hence to yonder place; and it shall remove,
> and nothing shall be impossible unto you. Howbeit this kind
> goeth not out but by prayer and fasting" (Matt. 17: 19-21)*

People can give you their opinion as to why God has allowed
certain things to happen, but if you want the real answer, just ask
God himself. I will never forget His answer that came to me in my
private place, my prayer room, (which is where I slept most of the
time for the first couple of years). God reminded me that just as I
was his, my son also belonged to him and He and only he had the
authority to take one of his. He allowed me to give birth to him.
He gave him to my husband and myself to care for, build memories
with, and watch him as he grew up to be a man. For almost forty
years we were blessed to have him, then God decided it was time
for him to go home. He had completed his purpose.

I asked God why he didn't take some of the people that didn't
seem to care about anything or anybody, that refused to give their
lives to him, and he answered by saying these words: when you
were in the world I kept you and protected you and gave you a
chance to come to me, why shouldn't I do the same for everyone
that do not know me yet? That's why I called you. You will go and
tell the world about me, tell them who I am so they will not have
an excuse in the end.

I can tell you, after that I have never asked God anymore
questions about that storm I was in. I just trust Him with what
I don't understand or things that I tell myself I don't understand.

How did I feel? I truly felt like His child that was in trouble and
had to turn to Him even though I felt hurt by my heavenly Father
and that He was the reasons for my pain. I was in such unbearable
pain and He had allowed it; but since I knew He loved me I still
turned to him, because I knew He would answer all my questions.

Have you ever cried silent tears? These are tears that no one
can see and no one can hear you crying. I thank God for the people

that he placed in my life because he knew what I would be going through and my family is and was about two thousand miles away. I felt that because I was a child of God and a minister, that I should understand and be able to accept these things. Was I in for a big surprise. Being a child of God and a minister does not exempt us from being human, having the same feelings as anybody else. If anything, our pain is even greater because of the compassion we have for those that have not yet accepted Christ as their Lord and Savior, and for the ones that are saved and the struggles they go through during the different seasons of their lives.

I learned that there is nothing wrong with grieving or letting others see you grieve for your loved one. Psalm 30: 5, it tells us that weeping may endure for a night but joy comes in the morning. Sometime our night may be long and seem as if it will never end, but if we hold on to His hand and our faith in Him, and wait on Him the change will come. Isaiah 40: ask the question;

> *"Hast thou not known? Hast thou not heard, that the everlasting God, the Lord the Creator of the ends of the earth, fainteth not, neither is he weary. There is no searching of his understanding. He giveth power to the faint, and to them that have no might he increaseth strength. Even the youths shall faint and be weary, and the young men shall utterly fall but they that wait upon the Lord shall renew their strength; they shall mount up with wings as eagles; they shall run, and not be weary; and they shall walk and not faint" (Isa. 40: 28-31).*

I knew in my spirit that God never makes a mistake, I knew that I was not really alone, and that he was there with me but I felt very alone at the time. I was thinking as a mother that had lost her only child and the pain was unbearable.

I can tell you that I don't know about anyone else but I know leaning and trusting totally in God *is what* got me through such a trying time. If it had not been for Him I would not have made it, I would not be here today to share my story with you. I was able to make it through the night because he gave me strength. As I went through I learned how to wait on him and trust him completely.

If you have not lost a child I cannot describe the pain to you, but I can tell you that I felt as if my insides had been pulled out, as if the umbilical cord was finally being cut with a dull knife and I felt empty inside. I could hear myself as I screamed and screamed but no one could hear me because the screams were silent. Everything inside me was crying for my child; sometime the silent tears would run down my face when I was in public but my lips never parted, my screams were only heard by God. Even though at the time it seemed as if God was not listening I knew he was and I knew he cared.

CHAPTER 19
The Visit

I wouldn't visit the grave site of my son while my family was still here, I don't know why that was, except for the fact that they looked so hurt and sad so I was trying to be strong for them. I realize now that I should have had support from someone that cared the first time I visited the grave site. I just didn't want to see the hurt in their eyes that I was feeling in my heart, plus I knew I would have to make that trip alone sooner or later.

Once I was alone I knew it was time for me to visit my son's grave. Since he was a veteran he was buried in the military cemetery on Ft Sam Houston. I kept telling myself he is not in that grave, yet I was having a very difficult time getting into my car and driving out to Ft Sam. I tried going every week but it was getting harder instead of easier. The cemetery was beautiful, all the headstones were neatly lined up in perfect order. I would often see people sitting on the ground beside the grave of their loved one's headstone. Some people would have chairs, and I don't know why but I would feel so sad for them.

Once when I went to the cemetery I found myself on my knees sobbing uncontrollably. I could hear myself telling Kenny that I was so very sorry that I couldn't help him. You see, I felt at the time that if I had prayed harder, or maybe prayed a different prayer he wouldn't have died, I felt that somehow it was my fault, that because I was a minister there should have been something I could have done. In my spirit I knew that it was time for him to go, that he had completed his mission on this earth, but the mother part of me felt that she had somehow let her child down.

As time went by it wasn't going to the cemetery that began to give me peace but it was staying focused on my purpose, the reason God called me became foremost in my mind. Prayer praise and worship and staying in his Word kept me going. God reminded me one day that the cemetery was not where my son was. It was a place where the headstone was placed in his memory. It was after that day that I began to go to the cemetery less and less. It was then that I knew without a doubt that I trusted My Heavenly Father, "The Great I AM.

I woke up one morning and the Holy Spirit directed me to turn to the 11th chapter of Hebrews verse 1, I had asked the Lord for a word for a friend and He gave me these verses; but as I read and re-read and begin to mediate on the verses God began to deal with me. He showed me that the scripture was not only for my friend but also for me. He began to reveal to me that my faith in Him was stronger than I knew and as long as I held on to that faith and trust, my love for Him, not only would I make it through the pain and heartache that I was going through now but I would continue to come through any valley, go over any mountain, weather any storm, walk through any season in my life because I could do all things through him.

I now had the reassurance and knew for sure and without a doubt that He was always with me not only to help me make it through this pain; but that He would turn my sorrow into joy and I would have that peace that surpasses all understanding. He reminded me that it was because of my faith and trust in Him, in his Word that I accepted his Son as my personal savior long ago. It is by faith that I believe His word is true. I have come this far by faith.

"Now faith is the substance of things hoped for the evidence of things not seen" (Heb., 11:1).

CHAPTER 20
Once a Mother Always a Mother

Whether we as mothers want to admit it or not, deep down we want our children to need us to a point. Maybe it's just to babysit sometime or they just need to talk, and want us to listen to their problems, or give advice that they may or may not take. Whatever they need us for we are glad we are there for them, that does not mean we always do everything they ask us to. I've come to the conclusion that children are supposed to always need their parents especially their mom.

After God took my son home I felt so alone, as if no one needed me anymore. But God being God, already knowing what was going to take place in my life had already placed two wonderful little boys in my life and would send more later, and what is even more wonderful when I look back is that he allowed my son to get to know the first two. As of today, I have a total of 7 wonderful, smart, talented young boys (did I say handsome also) that I love as if they were my own grandchildren and I thank God for their parents and grandparents for allowing me to have such an important role in their lives. Oh yes, and I have one little girl that is a little lady spelled with capital letters.

Love your children, cherish them, teach them to respect others and themselves. Most of all, teach them about God and how much He loves us all. The Bible clearly tells us to train up a child.

"Train up a child in the way he should go; and when he is old he will not depart from it"(Proverbs 22:6).

CHAPTER 21
Someone else is in his Room

My son has been gone for several years now. I had stopped writing my story, being obedient to God, I didn't understand it, I just obeyed, all He said was that there is something else, and I didn't understand. I thought I was doing good, I had accepted the fact that my son was gone and I was going on with my life, being led by the Holy Spirit. Then something happened that made me realize that I had not come to terms with it at all and God had to allow something to occur that would make me realize that there was still more pain I had not yet given to Him.

I received a phone call from my pastor saying that there was a lady in town that had no place to live and would I consider allowing her to stay with me until she got on her feet. I couldn't believe pastor had asked me to do this knowing I was a very private person plus I had never met this person. He told me to think about it so I said I would pray about it, and I would let him know. As I hung up the phone I was saying to myself, there is no way a stranger is coming into my home to live but God had other plans. As the day went on I begin to asked God what should I do, and at the same time I kept telling myself that there was no way I was going to do this, plus my family would have a fit. I could hear them yelling all the way in North Carolina. asking me if I was insane. I can tell you that God will have you doing things you would never do on your own, but just because He said do it you just be obedient.

Pastor called me later and asked if I would pick this lady up and take her to church on Sunday morning because she didn't have a car and I said I would. He gave me the phone number, name and address of the place she lived temporarily.

As I stood in my bedroom getting ready for church that Sunday morning God spoke to me so very clear and told me to do it. It was so clear and soft that I looked around knowing that I wouldn't see anyone. I called pastor and left a message telling him I had my answer from the Lord, that He said do it. So, now I was going allow this person that I had never met into my home to live.

After church that day we met with the pastor and decided on the arrangements, that she would move in on Wednesday. This would give me time to move some things around. What I didn't realize until that Sunday night was that this was God's way of making me face some things that I thought I had already faced.

You see, she was going to be staying in my son's bed room, the room he called his when he came to spend the night. All of his things were still in that room untouched. As I entered the room and began to move his things, it was as if he had just passed away and God was making me just push his things aside as though they didn't matter. Why was God making me relive this, why had he sent this woman whom no one knew, into my life to stay in my child's room, it was almost more than I could bare. I picked up the phone to call my pastor and his wife to come over, but God said no, at that point I put the phone down, and just sat down in the floor and started to cry heart wrenching tears. I sat in the floor and sobbed until I was tired. I remember saying to the Lord, I can't do this, then I started telling Him I can't do this without you God. At that point, I began asking him for the strength I would need to do this. I began piece by piece to move all my son's clothes and the flag that was draped over his coffin out of the room that I had called his for so long.

When I finished the room, it was completely empty, there wasn't anything to remind me of Kenny, the carpet had been cleaned even though it wasn't dirty, new curtains and bed linen had replaced the old.

There was a freshness about the room now, and it was as if a weight was lifted from me. I understood at that moment why God had sent this person into my life to live for a little while in what used to be my son's room. Now I could move forward. After that He began once again give me the words to complete this book.

> *"And we know All things work together for good*
> *to them that love God, to them who are the called*
> *according to his purpose"(Rom.8:28).*

CHAPTER 22
A Precious Bundle of Joy

Achild is a precious gift from God. They are to be shared with others, first with family and friends. As they grow their circle begin to grow larger and larger with people they meet. We begin to realize we are going to have to share them with the outside world, not something we are ever ready for. They will begin making friends outside the family and they will be included into their circle. We send them to school, crying on that first day but not letting them see us and by the time we get back home we realize that we don't have a choice anymore except to trust that they will select the right friends and hope and pray we have given them a solid foundation with the right values so they grow and learn how to survive in this world. Before we know it they are dating, out of high school and into college. My son decided to go into the Air Force and then college. We watch them grow up before our very eyes. Many times we are so involved in trying to raise them the right way we fail to thank God enough for giving them to us.

We are there for them as they go through their trials and try to help them not to make too many mistakes, knowing all the time that mistakes will be made because that is how one learn and grow. We pray that they have a good life and the good part will make the bad times seem not so bad.

As a Christian parent, you hope and pray that they will accept

Jesus Christ as their personal savior, that you have taught them the way that they should go and that they won't depart from it; praying that even when things are hard that they will still remember what they were taught.

We hope they will grow up to see us get old and gray, but if by chance it is God's will that they go first, thank God for the time you had with them. Cherish the happy times, laugh about the times they did something wrong and you had to punish him or her, and it hurt you as it hurt them even though they didn't believe it at the time. Many times they would come back and apologize, it may be a few years later but it still made us as parents feel good.

When their journey has come to an end down here, this gift that was given to us to love, nourish and share with others, they will return to the giver; the One that gave them to us for a while. He receives them back to Himself and they will have eternal life if they had accepted Christ as their personal savior.

You see, this journey has many seasons and many twists and turns. For some their journey is shorter than others. We hope they are with us for a long time but we don't know the plan nor the path that God has for them. My son completed his journey before I did, so God took him home. I had hoped that I would have had him with me longer but I realize I was blessed to have him for 39 years.

I have seen so many parents grieving over the last few years because they have lost their child at such a young age, and I say thank you God for allowing me to have my son for the time I did.

I think of Kenneth every day. He didn't always do as I wanted him to and he made some bad decisions along the way but haven't we all, but he made a lot of good choices also.

As for me I will continue working in the purpose in which God has called me until he takes me home. I have preached in many churches of different denominations and I have found that the people that belong to God and the ones that are hungry for the Word and even those that are curious will listen, and some will receive it if it is the Word of God and not watered down, and they believe the person delivering that Word is a vessel used by God.

We make a lot of choices on this journey, but the most important one any of us can make is to give our lives to Christ, to accept him as our personal Lord and Savior, then gladly accept our purpose that he calls us into.

CHAPTER 23
What I Have Learned/ Things I Have Shared

You may ask, what are some things I have learned from all of this? I have learned that when God brings us out of a storm, out of the valley of shadow of death we are stronger in Him. I've also learned that there is no doubt what so ever in my mind that God is real, that he watches over and protects his own. I learned that we must trust God even if we don't understand why he is allowing certain things to take place in our lives.

I know that I would not have made it through my pain and grief or anything else if it had not been for Him; He was and still is always with me, guiding, teaching and watching over me.

In my darkest hour God was with me; in my brightest hour, he is with me. I would not have been able to withstand the persecution or a "type of persecution" of being a minister in a Baptist church without His protection, without his strength. I say "would not have been " because I can truly say I pray for those that still do not believe, and the things that are said and done to destroy the character of one that has been called by God. When my character and integrity is attacked I just stand back and watch God as he builds it back up. I know I am protected by Him. I can tell you, he will fight your battles if you give them to Him.

I am not complaining, because everything that I have been through has just made me stronger, it has taught me how to lean and depend totally of God. I have learned how to stay focused on my purpose.

I have preached through the pain of losing my son. I never stopped being God's vessel, allowing Him to use me. When I would get up every morning I would yield myself to him and when I would get ready to go out the door I would say ok "God it's you and me" and I grew stronger in him and I am still growing in Him.

It has made me stronger in God because just knowing He will see me through anything gives me strength. Don't get me wrong now, there were some days when God had to give me a firm talk before I started my day. As a matter of fact, as I write this God still make me sit down at times and just listen to him. He is an awesome Father.

He has given me a deeper revelation of who He is. I have walked through the valley of shadow of death and God was there holding my hand, guiding me, protecting me, and cradling me in His arms when I needed to rest. He has restored me.

"Trust in the Lord, and do good; so shalt thou dwell in the land, and verily thou shalt be feed. Delight thyself also in the Lord and He shall give thee the desires of thy heart. Commit thy way unto the Lord; trust also in him; and he shall bring it to pass, and He shall bring forth thy rightness as the light, and thy judgment as the noonday. Rest in the Lord and wait patiently for him" (Ps. 37: 3-7).

In this book I have shared many things with you, the tears, the pain and heart ache of losing my son but I hope you have also listened as I shared with you the fact that I was and I am so happy and grateful to God for allowing me to have him for over thirty years.

When I think about all the parents that will never see their children grow up, never see them go to school or college, or on their first date, drive a car, I pray for them, asking God to give them strength and comfort that only He can give.

I had the privilege of watching him grow up to be a man. When I pray for those that have lost children and I also pray for the parents that have children, that your children will live long lives and that you always let them know you love them. For those that have lost children, hold on to the memories, hold on to God.

I hope and pray that this book will help you in some way. I'm so grateful I had a good relationship with my son. He would get upset with me sometime, and he did some things that we didn't approve of, but he always knew his father and I loved him.

"O magnify the Lord with me and let us exalt his name together. I sought the Lord, and he heard me, and delivered me from all my fears. Oh, taste and see that the Lord is good, blessed is the man that trusted in him" *(Ps. 34: 3-4, 8).*

Find and accept the purpose God has for you. There will be obstacles, but He will always be with you, just remember there is nothing too hard for God. I have shared with you my struggles with accepting my call to the ministry but I hope as you read you became aware of the joy and peace I found once I accepted my call, surrendered to God and became obedient to His will.

I hope you have listened as I shared with you the fact that I would not change the way God has directed my life; that he really does work things out for our good, we just have to learn to trust him. I have shared with you some of the pain I have felt as a minister of the gospel in a denomination where it is not the "norm" to be a woman minister, but I soon learned to count it all joy. Just knowing that God has chosen me, a little country girl from North Carolina to carry His Word is the greatest honor I could ever have and I won't complain. I have watched as man has put stumbling blocks in my path. God has shown me how to just step over them or He just lifts me over them. Every once in a while he allows me to watch and they fall over the very same stumbling block they had put in place for me. He always goes before me and prepare the way.

I just want to share with you another time I have shed tears. As I would stand and preach or teach or minister to others the Lord would show me how much many were suffering and not knowing which way to turn, and my heart would hurt when I didn't know if I had gotten through to them or not, then one-day God stopped me and told me to just preach the Word, just teach His Word, just minister to the people that He would send me to and He would touch the hearts of man and they will make a choice. In other words, all I needed to do was be obedient and do what He had called me to do.

I know that there are still many more mountains for me to climb and I will go through the valley again and again but I know for sure that God is always with me; that his goodness and mercy will follow me all the days of my life and one day I will go home also and dwell in his house forever.

The Bible tells us that one day there will be no more tears or pain and sorrow, that He will wipe all our tears away

"And God shall wipe away all tears from their eyes, and there shall be no more death, neither sorrow, nor crying neither shall there be any more pain, for the former things are passed away" (Rev. 21:4).

I have preached through the pain. I now preach without the pain but with a joy and peace I cannot explain. I have walked through the valley of shadow of death but I was never alone, God was always right there with me, protecting and leading me to a safe place. When I was too weak to go on He allowed me to rest for a little while as He renewed my strength.

When I say I have preached through the pain I don't mean that there aren't times when I don't feel sad or miss my son because I miss him all the time but the pain I used to feel so deep in my heart has been changed to a quiet sadness that God only allows me to feel sad for a little while then he gently reminds me of my purpose.

Another type of pain I used to feel the first few years after God called me into the ministry is gone, and I also shed tears over this because I realized that even though I was overjoyed that God had chosen me, this was in no way going to be an easy road to travel.

When we would visit other churches many times I would not be greeted, not even a hand shake because I was a minister. I couldn't understand why anyone, especially people of God refused to speak even when I greeted them first, just because they didn't agree with something God had done. But then I would remember how they treated the disciples because they preached the gospel. I preach that same gospel today.

> *"And, as they spake unto the people, the priest, and the captain of the temple, and the Sadducees, came upon them. Being grieved that they taught the people, and preached through Jesus, the resurrection from the dead. And they laid hands on them and put them in hold unto the next day for it was now eventide (Acts, 4:1-3).*

God has called many women into the ministry and He will continue to do so. If he used women in the Old Testament and He chose a woman to carry His Son and give birth to him, raise and love him how can we not be humbled and honored to carry the Word to the people no matter what some may say or how they treat us at times.

> *"In the beginning was the Word, and the Word was with God, and the Word was God. The same was in the beginning with God. And the Word was made flesh, and dwelt among us and we beheld his glory, the glory as of the only begotten of the Father, full of grace and truth. John (1:1-2,14).*

We have to remember how Christ was treated, how his prophets and the early Christians were treated. That is why I just smile when I'm not allowed in pulpits or sit with other ministers at times or not even greeted with a hand shake or hello, I just say thank you God for choosing and loving me.

You have seen this verse many times in this book because it is true. I can do all things through Christ who strengthens me' and so can you if you trust Him.

If you are reading this and haven't yet given your life to Christ, why don't you just try Him

If you are reading this and you need comfort, just trust him, He's a wonderful comforter. If your heart is broken or breaking, he will mend your broken heart. He's a healer if you need healing, if you just need someone to listen to all your problems, he's a good listener and there is no problem that he cannot solve if you give them to him. I Know my Purpose and he also has a purpose for you.

A Note:

You will always miss that special someone that God has taken home. I miss my son every day. There are times when I am reminded of something he did or said and it will make me smile. Then there are the special occasions, birthdays and holidays or the times when he would just drop by to say hi.

I know each of you have special times you remember, cherish the memories, keep them close to your heart, they will make you smile, at times maybe you will even shed a tear, and that's ok because one day all our tears will be wiped away by our father

During the process of writing "Preaching through the Pain" God healed my heart, taught me patience, also he taught me how to completely trust him, how to give my burdens to him and focus on what He had called me to do. He has anointed me to preach the gospel, to teach and minister to others. As I continue this journey, fulfilling my purpose that He has called me into, I have that peace that surpasses all understanding because he fights my battles for me. He will fight yours too if you give them to him.

God bless you.

Reverend Helen McBynum is a native of North Carolina, but has chosen San Antonio, Texas as her second home. She accepted her call to the ministry in 2004. She was licensed in 2005 and was ordained in 2006 by her pastor of her home church in San Antonio, of which she now the senior associate minister.

She received her education at Liberty University; she majored in Biblical studies with a minor in Christian Counseling. She is a member of the American Association of Christian Counselors. In addition to her responsibilities at her home church, being obedient to God she has a Nursing Home ministry where she preach and ministers to the clients and the employees every Sunday morning. She is totally committed to the purpose in which God has placed her.

Printed in the United States
By Bookmasters